CELLO
WORKING METHODS

IMPROVE FASTER
IN LESS TIME

This book is like no other. It won't teach you how to play the cello: there are dozens of effective methods for that. It will teach you how to practice the cello efficiently so that you can improve your cello as quickly as possible in the shortest time possible.

The miracle recipes that boast of making you play the cello in a few weeks and effortlessly will allow you to play one or two pieces of music. You will manage to please yourself in the short term by mimicking the experienced musician, but your learning will be superficial and you will not progress: you will give up very quickly, because you will never know the extraordinary satisfaction of true progress, the one that required work... This joy that you can see in the smile and eyes of a twelve-year-old child who, after an hour and a half of work bordering on tears, finally manages to overcome the difficulties and plays without error a piece that seemed inaccessible to him the day before.

Unfortunately, you have little time to play and you improve slowly. Also, when you learn a new piece, there is always a passage or two that you never manage to play properly, and because you insist on mastering the piece, you spend a lot of time on it for little result. And that frustrates you.

You've reached a threshold that you can't break through. And yet, it would be a shame not to reach a good instrumental level when you know the pleasure you can get out of it!

You have bought cello learning methods and you wonder if they are relevant.

The problem doesn't lie with the books you bought to learn how to play: they are all good. The problem is that you don't have the right working methods, because they are known

mainly by classical musicians who have attended the best classic music academy or best music schools.
However, these methods are rarely shared with musicians who have not been to these classic music schools.

The aim of this book is to show you very precisely how to work the cello in order to be efficient and progress as quickly as possible.

These techniques often give impressive results, but they also require hard work.

TABLE OF CONTENTS

Advices for motivation to play the cello 9
   Dissociate working the cello and playing the cello 10
   Law of Least Effort 12
   To watch your fingers or not to watch your fingers? 13
   Select the scores 13
   How often to play the cello per week and for how long? 14
   Warming up and working the sound of cello 17
   Vary musical style 20
   Is it necessary to learn to read music to play cello? 21
Cello Working techniques 23
   Imitate great cello players 24
   Shift the beginning of the piece at each session 25
   When you fail Accidentals 27
   Scribbling 28
   How to practice a difficult section in a piece ? 28
   Avoid degradation of a piece over time 31
   The work of musical nuances 32
   Boost your progression: face new challenges 32
   How to learn by heart? 34
Training to play the cello in front of an audience, or preparing competitions 37
   Marathon workout 38
   Discomfort zone techniques 42
The work of cello virtuosity 43
   Virtuosity is mastery 44
   Fingerings and positions on the cello 45
   The metronome's work of mastery and stability 45
   Working on sections where the notes are very fast 52
   Back-nibbling technique: for the ultra-difficult 54
   Regularity workouts for difficult sections 60
   Working on a difficult section: x3 x5 x8 repetition 63
   Use the metronome to learn difficult and long sections that include various rhythms 64
Cello-specific working tips 67
   Relaxation 68
   Separate hand work and open strings 68
   Left hand right hand coordination 69
   Play with the bow upside down 69
   Reverse all the bowings 69
Structure of a working session 71
Summary of techniques 77
Worksheets 83

ADVICES FOR MOTIVATION TO PLAY THE CELLO

DISSOCIATE WORKING THE CELLO AND PLAYING THE CELLO

In order to progress faster, you will have to make the difference between playing and working. Indeed, they are two different things that complement each other.

When we play, we enjoy ourselves, we listen to ourselves, we listen others if we play together. It can even correspond to moments of great happiness. We forget the daily routine and we create a personal bubble of joy.

However, in order to achieve this, a given technical skill level must be reached. And to reach this technical level, you have to practice the cello. This requires training your brain to control your fingers, and allowing your fingers to acquire certain automatisms and dexterity that will allow you to play.

To practice does not therefore consist in playing pieces, but in preparing and developing your brain and your fingers to play pieces that are more and more difficult to play and more and more satisfying to play.

This involves practicing chromatisms, arpeggios, sonority, scales. It also involves practicing your ear so that it learns to listen to others while you play. practicing means cutting the pieces into sections that you will have to work separately from each other in order to technically master them.

Many beginner musicians don't like to practice and want to skip steps: they only want to play.

However, practicing is essential, because there is no progression without work. What is less well known is that work can sometimes be as satisfying as playing: especially when you manage to master difficulties that you didn't think you could master.

It is always advisable to practice the music before playing it. Playing music will be the daily reward for your work. And by doing so, your level will quickly increase, which will give you even more pleasure. And this gradually turns into a virtuous circle:

You practice

⬇

your technical level increases

⬇

you can play more and more difficult and satisfying pieces

⬇

it motivates you to practice technique even more

LAW OF LEAST EFFORT

We are by nature lazy even if we are motivated. Surprisingly, a tiny detail can make it possible to practice more.

Leave your instrument as if you had been away for five minutes and are about to come back to play.

Leave your cello ready to play on a stand, as if you had been gone five minutes and are going to come back to play.

When you don't play, leave your cello on a stand in a place where it almost obstructs the passage, the aim is that you pass as much as possible in front of it while it is ready for use, and all you have to do is extend your hand to take your cello and play.

To make the work even easier, I advise you to keep your scores open on the right page on the music stand. So, invest in a music stand in the style of the Manhasset music stand, with gutter.

Indeed, it is very stable and has a very interesting detail: a gutter at the bottom. This way, the scores are placed on the music stand and you can put your metronome, pencil and eraser just below it in the gutter.

Thus, not having to install anything to begin will require less effort to start playing. And that's understandable: who wants to take three minutes to set up, find the right page, take their cello out of its case, all that to play for just ten minutes?
This little tip has a considerable influence on children and adults, especially beginners.

TO WATCH YOUR FINGERS OR NOT TO WATCH YOUR FINGERS?

Try not to look at your fingers when you play. This will of course be very difficult if you are a beginner, but it will also help you to progress more quickly.
You will be able to follow the score much more easily without having to constantly raise and lower your head, so you won't get lost while playing. By staying focused on the score, you will make fewer mistakes and progress faster.

SELECT THE SCORES

Don't try to do the unachievable: the musical progression must be gradual.
If you think the piece is too difficult, set it aside to work on it later. Go back to simpler pieces that you will be able to play correctly from beginning to end (even if it requires practice).

The simplest way to do this is to rely on traditional learning methods, which are usually very well designed to rank the pieces in order of increasing difficulty.

Finally, one last piece of advice regarding the choice of pieces: if you are a beginner to intermediate level, don't choose pieces that are too long because it is difficult to motivate yourself when it is too long, and you may not be able to master it all.

HOW OFTEN TO PLAY THE CELLO PER WEEK AND FOR HOW LONG?

In order to progress, you have to practice. In principle, the more you practice, the more you will progress.

Indeed, there is a concept called the "experience curve" which says that you improve by a constant percentage every time you double the amount of work you have accumulated". This means that you will improve by the same percentage when you go from 1 to 2 hours of cumulative work, then 2 to 4, 4 to 8, 16, 32, 64, 128, 256, 512, 1024 hours, etc.

However, music is rarely a priority in an often overloaded daily life and, fortunately, musical progression is not as mathematical as described above: practicing, but efficiently, will allow you to improve. The way you divide the work during the week will give very different results.

It is tempting not to practice too much during the week and try to compensate during the weekend. That's why some people only play their instrument once or twice during the week, but play 1.5 hours on Sundays.
In reality, in order to progress, it is more important to play every day a little, rather than once a week, and it is even better to practice 7 times 10 minutes than 1.5 hours at a time.

Let's see why.
Mastering instrumental technique requires your brain to memorize reflexes: combinations of fingers, sequences of hand movements, body position.
The problem is that the brain is primarily designed to forget and get rid of useless information. On the contrary, creating lasting reflexes requires the creation of neural networks, i.e. the creation of brain matter. This is very energy-intensive and our brain does not like it very much. This is why, whatever the learning process, the brain puts the information into its short-term memory and waits to find out if it is useful to remember the information. Playing only every two or three days, or worse once a week, tells your brain that it is not worth remembering the information. Indeed, why spend so much energy to store knowledge and reflexes that will only be used once or twice a week?
No interest. As a result, the learning efforts you make once a week, however intense, are largely lost.
On the other hand, if you play even a little every day, your brain has no choice but to consider your learning a priority since you have to use your new skills every day.

If practicing is essential, it is a long-term job. It will also require perseverance. There will be periods when you will suffer: you will not progress, you will be demotivated, you will no longer be interested in playing. These non-progressing periods are normal and you must persist, because these milestones are part of learning: they allow you to unconsciously digest the knowledge you have already acquired.

In conclusion, play every day and be persistent. And if you don't have the time, play for even 5 to 10 minutes: it's not a waste of time, it's just that you are anchoring the reflexes in your brain.

WARMING UP AND WORKING THE SOUND OF CELLO

A good routine is to start by warming up with technical exercises.
Take 5 minutes to play
- chromatic scales,
- classic scales
- and arpeggios

It is recommended that you do at least one exercise to improve the sound of your cello. In general, these are all exercises that you should play very slowly as you listen to yourself. Exercises of this type are there to improve your sound. Play as slowly as necessary to hear yourself and correct your sound.

Hold music notes

A good exercise is to go up a scale very slowly by linking the notes in pairs, starting with the last note.
This gives exercises in the following style:

Listen to yourself and become aware of how your body feels when you produce a high-quality sound. You will then seek this same sensation in more complex scores, and the sound should follow with the same quality as in slow work.

The half bow

To improve sound quality, play a theme using only half or two-thirds of the bow. This is of course not a habit to get into, but an exercise that will help you improve your sound.

Playing with half bow is important to solve a problem that is encountered at any level: the problem of playing **systematically** with the whole bow.

However, depending on the duration of the notes, you should not always use the whole bow to obtain a beautiful sound. Indeed, if you always play with the whole bow, you risk sometimes having notes that are not very dense because you put too much speed and not enough pressure.

Moreover, playing with half the bow requires a very good contact point between the bow hair and the string: therefore a richer sound.

Listen to yourself via a microphone

A good tip is to play in front of a quality microphone, with a headset in which you listen to your own sound without being able to hear it yourself directly. You hear the sound your listeners might hear, and you can then correct it much more easily.

Be careful not to do this work too often: the aim is to become aware of your weaknesses, but you risk focusing too much on what is wrong, rather than focusing on what you can improve. That is why it is **sufficient** to do this once a month.

VARY MUSICAL STYLE

You probably are interested in one style of music or another: classical, baroque, rock or even metal.

Each style encounters its own particular difficulties that are unique to it and that are found little or not at all in other musical styles.

To progress faster, you must constantly face new difficulties, and one way to do this is to play a piece from a very different repertoire into your favorite repertoire.

Each of these new difficulties will help you to progress in your favorite repertoire.

If you love hard rock, the dexterity and virtuosity of classical music (scales and arpeggios included) will help you to improve your virtuosity which will help you in Hard rock.

Conversely, practicing some Hard Rock solos when you're into classical music can be fun and will provide different technical challenges.

Finally, playing unknown repertoires may help you discover pieces that you love and that you never imagined you would play.

IS IT NECESSARY TO LEARN TO READ MUSIC TO PLAY CELLO?

Many people say it is not necessary to learn to read music to play cello.

But just as it is possible to function in everyday life even when you can't read a text, it becomes difficult as soon as you are confronted with something new.

Learning to read music can be hard work, but it opens doors and musical landscapes that are otherwise inaccessible to you. So it would be a real shame to start off with such a handicap. There are many methods to learn to read notes. In France, the most famous handbook is "Dandelot", chose the older edition.

DANDELOT

Manuel pratique

POUR L'ÉTUDE DES CLÉS
SOL FA UT

EDITIONS MAX ESCHIG

Don't be impressed, it's much easier to learn to read music than to learn to read!

CELLO WORKING TECHNIQUES

IMITATE GREAT CELLO PLAYERS

Browse and listen to recordings of the pieces you want to play and try to imitate them (even if you play slower). This will help you to progress much faster, because you will know instantly how the piece should sound, in what style it should be played and, above all, you will understand the state of mind in which it should be played: calm? Overexcited?

Let's go even further: try to imitate the great soloists, their phrasing, their interpretation. Playing this acting game may seem ridiculous to you, but it will inspire you and reduce your chances of making basic interpretation mistakes. Do not hesitate to be caricatural in this work. This will force you to subconsciously analyse and better understand the piece you are playing.

Important note: when you imitate great cello players, it does not mean that you have to imitate them in their speed of execution. Play at a speed where you are comfortable so that each note is audible: the result should never be messy.

In conclusion, don't seek perfection, but imitate as closely as possible professional cello players: this will help you.

SHIFT THE BEGINNING OF THE PIECE AT EACH SESSION

When you have a long piece to play, there is a tendency to return naturally to the beginning of the piece at each new working session. As a result, the endings of pieces are often the least practiced.

There are two possibilities to solve the problem:

1. If your piece is 5 pages long, chunk it into 10 half pages and practice only half a page per session. At each session, don't play anything that has already been practiced, but start directly from the half page planned for your session. Then, during a session, you will chunk the half-page into one- or two-bar sections.
2. Another possibility, which will make it easier for you to focus on the half page of the day: rather than practicing the half pages from the first half page to the last half page, work backwards: practice the last half page first, then go up one half page at each session.

Finally, if the piece presents a wide variety of difficulties, chunk it into difficult and less difficult sections, and always practice the difficult sections first. Keep the easier sections for days when you are not very motivated, or when you have little time.

I suggested chunking the piece into half-pages, but if you are familiar with the notion of musical phrases, prefer to chunk your piece respecting the musical phrases. The half-page is therefore only a rough indication: the aim is to chunk the piece into sections that you will be able to practice correctly in a half an hour maximum.

Sometimes the difficulty of a piece is so great that it is only possible to practice a line or two in half an hour. In that case, don't be frustrated: on the contrary, if you overcome the difficulties, it will indicate that you are progressing quickly.

Last but not least, when you practice sections (or musical phrases) separately, it will not be easy to link the phrases together. Indeed, you will have to practice the transitions between the different sections of the piece. For example, play the 3-4 bars at the end of a half page, with the 3-4 bars of the next half page.

You may not play the piece from beginning to end for a few days or even weeks. But once you have practiced the different sections well, and practiced the transitions between sections, you will be able to play the piece from beginning to end easily.

WHEN YOU FAIL ACCIDENTALS

For every piece you play, you certainly have a key signature (and it will be worth a look before you play to see how many sharps (#) or flats (b) are present), but you also have accidentals i.e. unanticipated sharps, flats, or naturals.
So far, a priori, nothing very annoying. The small problem is that an accidental is considered valid during a whole bar without having to be indicated again.

The score is written as in A, but must be played as in B.

At first glance, nothing special. However, at all levels, even at very advanced levels, it is very easy to forget accidentals for many reasons :
- Lack of concentration.
- Non-tonal musical phrase that could work with or without accidentals if you rely only on your musical ear.
- A mistake while reading the music that you can't get rid of.

There is a simple way to solve this problem: for each accidental you fail twice, you mark the accidental with a pencil in as many places as you need to avoid making the mistake again. This way, your score will look like version B above. This is an unglorious, but effective way to solve this problem once and for all.

SCRIBBLING

In general, do not hesitate to write, circle and cross out on your score. Anything that can help you can be written down. This is not cheating.

HOW TO PRACTICE A DIFFICULT SECTION IN A PIECE ?

Regardless of a musician's level, everyone is confronted, at his or her own level, with difficulties that require to practice specifically the musical section: this is a problem that every musician has to deal with.

First of all, the type of difficulty must be defined.

Some difficulties are due to the speed of execution, which means that your fingers have difficulty executing the orders of your brain at the right speed. In that case, there are exercises that allow you to progress very quickly and overcome these difficulties (see the corresponding chapter). In the next example, notes are not difficult to read, but speed requires practicing with the appropriate techniques.

Example of a piece without any difficulty of reading but difficult to play :

Suite 4 for Cello Solo

JOHANN SEBASTIAN BACH
BWV 1010

Präludium

Some of the difficulties are related to the fact that you don't understand the music that is written or that it is very difficult to read: the rhythm is complex and there are accidentals everywhere.

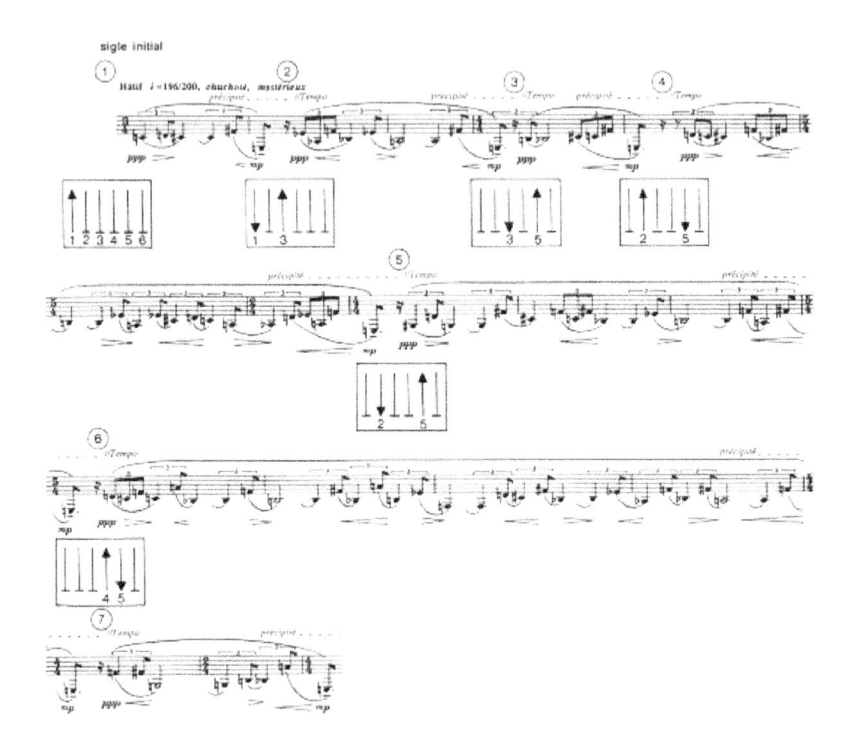

AVOID DEGRADATION OF A PIECE OVER TIME

You have practiced one piece, a second, a third... and after a few months or years, you realise that your real repertoire is limited to the last 2 or 3 pieces learned (or just the last one for some?).

This is very common.

This can be very frustrating and could even lead to discouragement to abandon the cello.
If you could have a cumulative musical progression, it would be nice, wouldn't it? Every new piece you learn would be an additional piece, not just the current piece you will soon forget.

There's really no secret: you have to maintain all your old pieces.
And the recipe is simple: play each of your old pieces 3 times in a row at least once a month. Even if you only play a maximum of one old piece a day, you will still have a repertoire of 30 songs! That's already very impressive!

In the case of very difficult pieces, at the limit of your technical level, in addition to playing them every month, it is useful to practice them entirely for the passages that you can no longer master (practice these passages at least once a quarter (it is only 4 times a year!).

THE WORK OF MUSICAL NUANCES

First of all, don't worry about the nuances at the early stages of learning a piece and play without worrying about them. By default, play everything loud enough.

Then, when you technically master the piece, add the nuances and caricature them. Feel that your **_forte_** is too loud, and your **_piano_** is almost inaudible. It will then be time to adjust the level if necessary.

BOOST YOUR PROGRESSION: FACE NEW CHALLENGES

Challenging yourself means playing new pieces, or sometimes choosing a piece that you feel is a little too difficult for you.

Record yourself in order to share your video on social networks or just to show it to your family. You are likely to make more mistakes than usual because of stress: this is normal and it is a powerful way to force yourself to play well. Remember where you made the mistakes, they are usually made in the parts where you are technically more fragile. Indeed, without stress, you play these sections without difficulty, but with stress, you have more difficulty: these are the sections you should practice first.

Recording yourself will force you to concentrate and will automatically increase your level of expectations even without you noticing it.

Even better, try to play in front of a real audience, even if it's only a very small audience of 3 or 4 people: your motivation and progress will automatically increase.

Variation of this challenge: if you have no audience and you live on the ground floor or first floor: play with the window wide open so that the whole street can hear you. You won't have a choice: you will have to play well so you don't sound ridiculous.

Anyway, whether during a recording or in front of an audience, if you make mistakes, you must :
- NEVER wince at your own mistakes! Because the vast majority will not hear your mistake, but will see your wince!
- Smile: those who will have heard a mistake will have a doubt: did they hear it right if you look so happy? And that's it!
- Continue as if nothing had happened and never go back.

Finally, never get angry when you encounter difficulties. On the contrary, every difficulty you encounter is a mini challenge that will make you progress even faster. Indeed, it is not by succeeding in something you already master that you will progress, it is on the contrary when you are confronted with difficulties that seem insurmountable. Thus, you will progress faster by practicing 5 ultra-difficult bars, rather than by learning a new, very easy 3-page piece. Why is this so? Because it will force you to progress on a technical level.

Indeed, the more you progress technically, the more you will be able to enjoy yourself while playing.

HOW TO LEARN BY HEART?

You may not like it, but one way to progress faster is to learn the pieces by heart.

Playing a piece by heart and playing a piece by reading a score are two really different things, a different way of looking at things. Learning by heart is often a long process, but the piece of music becomes better imprinted in your fingers and in your brain. On the other hand, when you know a piece by heart, you tend to play it more often, and you are often more comfortable.

How do you learn pieces by heart? In contrast to technical workouts, learning should be done by musical phrases, or chunks of musical phrases, and not by bar. When the phrases are long, you chunk them in smaller part, but the last note you play have to be the first note of a bar.

Let's imagine that you want to learn this phrase by heart:

As the phrases are long, the piece has to be chunked into sections.

First, chunk in sections of 9 notes (each box contains 9 notes) that you will have to learn by heart.

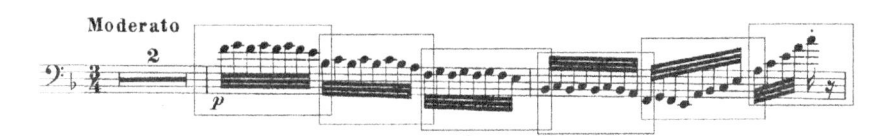

Then in sections of 17 notes that you will have to learn by heart as well.

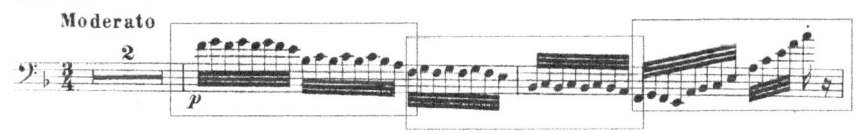

You enlarge the sections and you play them by heart:

To finally play the whole line by heart.

If you continue, you'll realize that the second line is identical to the first one: you can continue directly to the third line

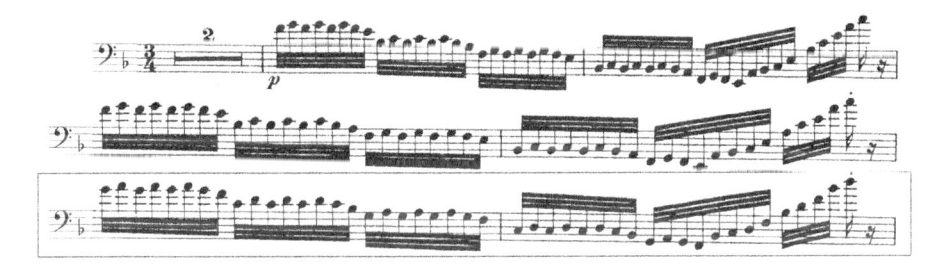

TRAINING TO PLAY THE CELLO IN FRONT OF AN AUDIENCE, OR PREPARING COMPETITIONS

MARATHON WORKOUT

If you have to perform in front of an audience, you will have to do something that you rarely do in your daily work: both because you probably only play a short time without interruption and because you are not confronted with stress.

However, one factor is often forgotten in preparation: endurance. In front of an audience, you have to play longer than usual and you have to remain focused.

If you are not prepared to improve your endurance, you risk unpleasant surprises, as you cannot stop and start again in front of an audience. As a result, new difficulties may appear, difficulties that are invisible in the usual daily practice.

I propose a marathon that will make you gain a lot in confidence and endurance. The aim is to tire you voluntarily until you find it difficult to focus and until playing becomes physically difficult. This will force you to solve problems you didn't have before, and that will almost automatically appear with some stress.

Prerequisite: to start a marathon, it is necessary that you already master your piece, i.e. that you are able to play it from beginning to end at least once without error.

Workout 1 (3 days in a row)

You play the piece 5 times in a row without ever stopping, even if you make mistakes.

Whole piece x 5 without interruption

Try to keep in mind the parts of the piece that you are having problems with: they will need to be practiced more specifically or as a priority. Beware, some mistakes are only made because of fatigue and lack of concentration: these mistakes are practiced by playing marathons. Once you have mastered workout 1. You can try workout 2.

Workout 2

Workout 2 is to be done once or twice a week maximum, when workout 1 has been done at least three times.

> Suite 4 for Cello Solo
>
> ## Whole piece
> ## x 5 minimum without interruption
> ## you stop only when you succeed
> ## 3 times in a row without error
> (maybe you will have to play 20 times in a row!)

Note that this technique is most effective with pieces in which there are few bars of silence. If you play a piece with several bars of silence spread throughout the piece, the marathon is less necessary.

In any case, the marathon should follow the following rule :

> **If you make mistakes, you must continue the piece <u>without going back</u> to repeat the bars where you made the mistakes. You have to imagine that you are playing with an orchestra that will not wait for you.**

DISCOMFORT ZONE TECHNIQUES

In preparation for competitions or in preparation for playing in front of an audience, it is necessary to prepare yourself by moving out of your comfort zone. For this, there are two techniques recommended at an advanced level (if you are a beginner to intermediate level, you are not concerned by these techniques).

Staircase technique

Run up and down the stairs three times on two floors before playing your piece without interruption and without error. This will make your heart rise as if you were under stress. Maybe your fingers will sweat···

Cold start technique

Play your piece without warming up at an unusual playing time
(when you wake up, without having had breakfast, or late in the evening when you are really very tired).

These techniques can put you in a situation of sufficient fatigue, stress and discomfort for you to verify how well you really master the piece. In addition, your heart will beat at least as fast as when you are stressed, which will allow you to mimic the conditions of a concert or competition as closely as possible. These extreme techniques should be used only when there is a high stake.

THE WORK OF CELLO VIRTUOSITY

VIRTUOSITY IS MASTERY

It is very impressive to see some musicians playing extremely fast. To be a virtuoso is not to play to the maximum of your technical ability, but to play well below your maximum tempo to have the most total control of what you are doing. Accuracy is then such that it seems fast when otherwise it seems messy.

To illustrate my point, that is not cello, but a violin player declared himself to be the fastest in the world, before becoming the laughing stock of professional and amateur celloists. Indeed, his performance is messy, not all the notes are played and not all the notes are audible. Here is the Youtube link (https://bit.ly/2violin) to a video that criticizes this, entitled "The World's fastest (and most inaccurate) celloist! ». Conversely, listen to celloist Kavakos: when questioned, Kavakos says he felt like he was playing slowly (youtube https://bit.ly/kavakos5).
So, don't be impressed by speed. Speed only makes sense when it is perfectly mastered: it is then called virtuosity.

Speed + Control = Virtuosity

Speed **without** control = yeks!

To practice your virtuosity, you have to practice slowly. For example, when you have difficulties in a piece, the first reflex should be to slow down... a lot. The slower the better.

FINGERINGS AND POSITIONS ON THE CELLO

In order to gain in virtuosity, you cannot afford to change position every time you play a complex passage. You need to think about what will be most effective and write down the positions or fingerings above the notes. Then don't change them and always play with the same fingerings.

THE METRONOME'S WORK OF MASTERY AND STABILITY

The metronome is judged by many as an instrument of torture. On the contrary, it should be your great friend. Indeed, the perception we all have of the speed at which we play is only a perception.
There is a natural tendency to speed up, sometimes a lot, in easy sections, and a natural tendency to slow down (sometimes a lot) in difficult sections.

Now, regularity in tempo will make the difference between a piece that is well played and a piece that sounds a little shaky. You should therefore not allow yourself any unwanted fluctuations in tempo. Moreover, if your regularity in tempo is perfect, it can mask a false note: in fact, if you don't slow down, don't hesitate and don't make a horrified face at the moment of a false note, there's little chance that your audience will hear it!

The metronome at a much slower speed than final speed

You can use the metronome at a very slow speed compared to normal speed. This allows you to retain your fingers and consolidate your control.

For pieces that are already mastered, it is useful to practice the metronome very slowly once in a while. Indeed, a piece that has already been mastered may be played by reflex, without having to think, especially in the fast parts. This should be avoided, and to regain control of the fingers, it is useful to play it with the metronome very very slowly (twice as slow is a good speed). This prevents a piece from deteriorating over time.

The metronome at a much faster speed than final speed

There is a proverb that says "who can do more, can do less". When you have mastered a piece, but feel you are at the limit of your ability at the expected tempo, practice with the metronome at a speed just a little faster (for example 92→96 or →102). This will help ensure that you can keep the normal tempo, as you will be a bit slower than you are able to do.

There is another reason to practice much faster than you want: when you play in front of an audience or if you have to play in competitions, you will be under stress and you will tend to find it difficult to hold your fingers back because you will feel like you are playing slower than you should. Chances are you will find yourself playing faster than you had planned: by practicing this on the metronome before a concert, you will have already experimented and practiced this excessive speed and you will know how to manage it: this will avoid the classic catastrophe of the cello player who accelerates because of stress and who fails pathetically from the beginning to the end of the piece.

If you practice very fast, you will have to play regularly with a metronome very slowly to keep control of your fingers.

The metronome at normal speed

Depending on the changing difficulty of a piece, you may accelerate in the easy passages and slow down in the difficult ones. This is perfectly natural. The metronome is the only means of verification. Mark the passages where you should go faster, or on the contrary slower, possibly annotate them with a pencil. Practice using the metronome until you no longer feel that you have to constantly speed up or slow down.

The uncomfortable speed metronome

That's it, you are more or less at ease with your piece at a very precise speed at the metronome, for example ♩=100. However, you start playing on reflexes, which doesn't allow you to progress while you want to gain mastery.

Set your metronome 2-3 notches lower, ♩=92 if you are comfortable at ♩=100. This speed a little below the normal speed but not too much is particularly uncomfortable to play and it will create many problems that you will have to solve. This will allow you to gain control.

The metronome on long values and off-beats for experts

The technique should only be used by advanced cello players: it is far too difficult for beginners to intermediate levels. It involves practicing the metronome successively with one pulse every:
1. eighth note
2. quarter
3. half
4. whole note

but by shifting the pulse so that it falls on upbeats.

Below, the pulses of the metronome are indicated by a « v ».

8th :

1/4 :

1/2 :

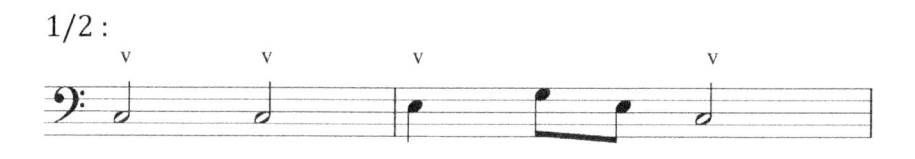

Whole note :

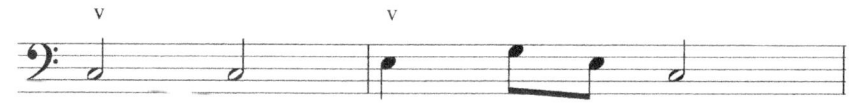

This work requires a good mastery of note values and forces to master the phrasing.

Expert level

Much more difficult: playing with a metronome in permanent off-beat. Above the musical stave "v": the 8th. Below the stave, the beats are every quarter, but shifted by one 8th, which means that everything is played off-beat. You have to beat the line above (very difficult).

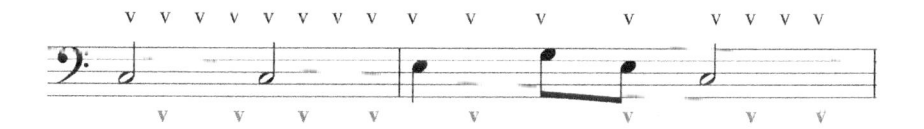

Practicing metronome with off-beat beats requires perfect mastery of the piece. However, this is for experts.

The metronome replaced by the left-right feet

It is obviously not possible to practice with the metronome all the time.
Use your feet to beat time. However, the foot beat must always be done by alternating left and right feet and not by beating the time always with the same foot. This allows the speed to be stabilised much more than with one foot and creates a swing that allows the pulse to be felt much more intimately. This makes this way of beating the time with your foot very effective when you play in an orchestra or chamber music ensemble.

Is it useful to say that kicking must absolutely be invisible to the public? The kick should be made with the toes inside the shoe, and almost imperceptible at the heel. The worst thing: kicking on the floor to make the floor vibrate! The audience will quickly feel the urge to kill you. And it doesn't matter what style: play without kicking your foot. The rule of the game is simple: you must never be seen kicking your foot (you must do it in great secrecy).

CONTROL AND STABILITY BY WORKING THE SLURS

The control and stability required for virtuosity is usually practiced with rhythm exercises, but it is very useful to add some stabilisation work through slurs.
Here are the combinations of slurs that you can practice on a piece (and this can also be practiced on scales and arpeggios).
This is a **very important** exercices in order to improve.

WORKING ON SECTIONS WHERE THE NOTES ARE VERY FAST

You have a difficult passage to practice and it is mostly very fast notes. You need to gain speed and stabilization ....
All the rhythmic work that is going to be presented can be practiced with or without a metronome.

First workout, when you are not familiar with the notes :

5 times (very long - very short)

5 times (very short - very long)

Once you've mastered the notes, here's a rhythm to stabilise your fingers and control their speed: this will allow you to play faster.

5 times (2 very long - 2 very short)

5 times (2 very short - 2 very long)

BACK-NIBBLING TECHNIQUE: FOR THE ULTRA-DIFFICULT

When it is necessary to play a phrase that is very difficult to play, because the sequences of notes are unusual and do not fall easily under the fingers, a back-nibbling technique should be used. This is an extreme technique intended for advanced levels when a phrase is so technically difficult that it will require huge amount of work. This is a technique for mastering particularly difficult and long phrases, especially when they are very fast. Let's take the following musical phrase as an example:

The first step is to chunk the sentence into shorter sections to be practiced separately. The section AB seems obvious, because there is an eighth note which allows you to recover your momentum in the sentence.

Then the section starting from B to the end. However, B to the end is a bit long: you will practice the BC and C sections to the end separately.

A major problem with long and difficult phrases is that the endings of the phrases are often practiced less than the beginnings. As a result, you will make more mistakes at the end of phrases, especially if there is a pressure to perform in front of an audience or if you want to record yourself.

Back-nibbling will allow more control at the end of phrases. Indeed, this technique requires you to master the ends of sentences before practicing the beginnings. You start from the end and work your way back to the beginning of the phrase little by little.

It works as follows:
- you play the last two notes of the sentence as quickly as possible (A).
- you play (A) again and you will do it again until you succeed 3 times in a row without error at the right speed (the one you want to reach)

You passed for (A). It was easy, because it was only two notes: you'll see that the game is going to be more and more difficult.

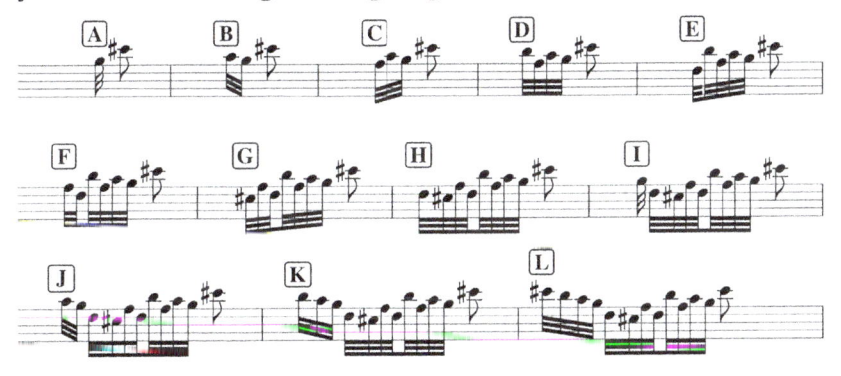

- You add a note to (A) (watch (B)).
- you play (B) as quickly as possible.
- you play (B) again and you will do it again until you succeed 3 times in a row without error at the right speed (the one you want to reach)

You passed for (B). You can start (C).

You do the same thing again, but with the last four notes instead of three (C). You passed 3 times in a row (C)? You can move on to (D). And so on.... You will play D, E, F, G, H, I, J, K and L.

When you have passed (L) three times in a row, you can consider that you have mastered your section of phrase (AB) below.

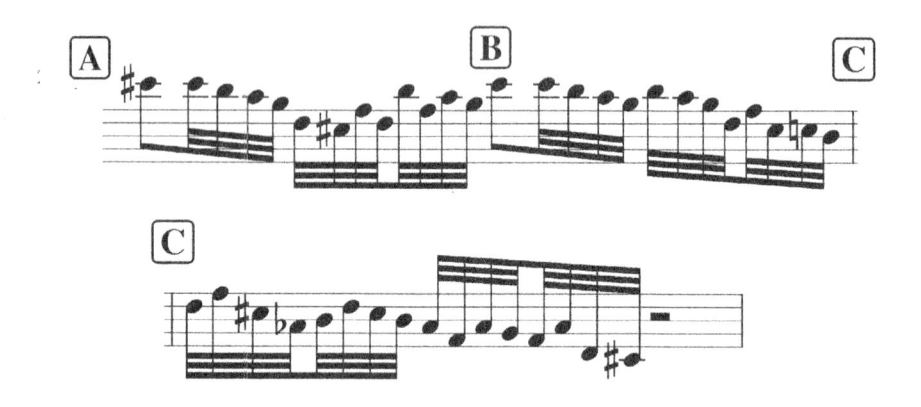

You will follow the same logic as before for the sentence sections (BC) then (C at the end).

As BC and C to end follow one another, you will practice ending from B to the end without stopping.

Each section must be completed 3 times consecutively before proceeding to the next one.

Next page: the score of what is to be played, line by line when you practice (B at the end) and when you have already mastered (C to end).

LEVEL N

LEVEL N+1

Extra rule for better finger control

For each line where you do not succeed 3 times consecutively correctly in the first 10 reps, you move back one level.

For example, if you were at **level N+1**, you go back down to **LEVEL N**.

REGULARITY WORKOUTS FOR DIFFICULT SECTIONS

There is nothing more unpleasant than someone who plays by accelerating and slowing down according to the difficulty of a piece. It is important that you manage to keep a high degree of regularity.

For this, your first great friend, whom you must love, is of course the metronome. But it will serve you above all to realise that your speed fluctuates, or that you don't play at the right speed.

Using the metronome is more than enough when what you are playing is rather easy.

However, if you have something difficult and long to play, it is necessary to know some techniques that can improve control and regularity of your speed.

The principle is simple: you have to alternate fast and slow speed: this will force you to control your fingers.

Here are the rhythms to use:

4 notes courtes, 4 longues

4 notes longues 4 courtes

Here is an example. If you need to practice a phrase like this ...

To gain in regularity, here are the two possibilities:

4 short 4 long

4 long 4 short

Then you can further improve your regularity by shifting the fast and slow notes :

2 long notes, then 4 short 4 long notes

WORKING ON A DIFFICULT SECTION: X3 X5 X8 REPETITION

To validate a difficult passage, it is necessary to succeed in playing the difficult passage correctly several times in a row.

The more advanced you are, the higher the number of successful repetitions must be.

- Beginner to intermediate level: succeed 3 times in a row.
- Intermediate to advanced level: succeed 5 times in a row.
- Above the advanced level: succeed 8 times in a row.

Matches can be used to visualize the progress of the work (any object in fact). Place 3 matches on the right side of your music stand. When you succeed, one match goes to the left. Each time you fail, all the matches go back to the right and you start again from scratch.

For beginners, this exercise can be frustrating. In that case, you can use the "3 times slow a day" instead.
 (three times slowly per day).

In any case, if you do not succeed, it means that you have to rework the section to master your fingers.

USE THE METRONOME TO LEARN DIFFICULT AND LONG SECTIONS THAT INCLUDE VARIOUS RHYTHMS

If you are dealing with a difficult piece or a very difficult section that is a bit long, but in which the rhythm is varied, the techniques previously presented will be impossible to use. You will practice using the metronome, using two possible methods.

Method 1: Simple and rather short method

1. Read the whole piece very slowly for the first time to understand how it works and to read the notes.
2. Look at the speed at which the piece is to be played. For example ♩=100
3. Set your metronome to ♩=50, which is half the speed (if you have time, you can even start at ♩=40). Play the section to be practiced at this speed.
4. When you manage to play the difficult passage three times in a row at this speed, increase the speed of the metronome.
5. Between 50 and 100, go through the metronome steps: ♩=56. ♩=66. ♩=76. ♩=84. ♩=92. ♩=100

   In general, the more difficult it is to achieve the metronome speed three times in a row, the slower you can increase it. So, don't hesitate to add an intermediate step if the speed is fast for you: for

example, add ♩=80 to avoid going directly from ♩=76 to ♩=84.
6. For each of these speeds, you must manage to play the entire section without error three times in a row.

Method 2: the +10-5 method

It is a more complex method than the previous one and it takes more time but it allows you to stabilize your fingers and your control at the same time as you increase the speed.

As before, you start from a low speed. For example, ♩=50
Then you go up by adding 10, then subtracting 5, then adding 10, etc. This will give the following speeds:

> ♩=50 → 60 → 55 → 65 → 60
> → 70 → 65 → 75 → 70 → 65
> → 75 → 70 → 80 → 75 → 85
> → 80 → 90 → 85 → 95 → 90
> → 100 → 92 (your objective)

You'll realise that it is especially when you are shifting into -5 speed that you will have the most difficulty, as it is harder to contain and control your fingers than to let them go.

CELLO-SPECIFIC WORKING TIPS

Although the purpose of this book is to give working and organization techniques, here are some tips and techniques specific to the cello.

RELAXATION

In general: all exercises should be done with the body as relaxed as possible, without losing energy by twisting the jaw, stretching the neck, or curling the toes. Easy to say, difficult to do...

SEPARATE HAND WORK AND OPEN STRINGS

Play open strings to listen to the quality of the sound without having to worry about the left hand. Pay particular attention when changing strings or bowing. Don't hesitate to practice sections "open-string": you don't use your left hand but you play with the right hand with the same gestures and pressure as if the left hand was playing (while resting).

Conversely, play only with the left hand, singing the melody aloud. The right hand can be on the strings but without an instrument it is also possible: on the arm or any other surface in fact. This is simply a matter of activating the neurons responsible for the movement of the fingers in a context where no sound can be obtained.

LEFT HAND RIGHT HAND COORDINATION

Here are two exercises to improve your coordination between your left and right hands:

1) Play right hand only when the left hand is ready. This causes gaps between each note, but it makes you aware of the possible delay between your hands and forces you to practice coordination.
2) Playing at the extreme tip of the bow is also a good exercise.

PLAY WITH THE BOW UPSIDE DOWN

The big problem with the bow is that it is much lighter at the tip than at the screw. In addition, at the screw, there is all the weight of the arm making pressure on the string, so there is less pressure at the tip.

Holding the bow upside down makes you aware of this difference: you have to play unevenly with pressure to get the same sound. This forces you to give more energy and weight to the tip (without getting tensed).

REVERSE ALL THE BOWINGS

Play by reversing all upbows and downbows. You will become aware of the upbows (which become downbows during the exercise).

When returning to the normal upbows and downbows, be careful not to make a decrescendo when going towards the tip or a crescendo when going back towards the screw.

STRUCTURE OF A WORKING SESSION

Routine session structure

Establishing a working routine can help you to progress a lot.
Here is a standard routine you can follow…

Warm-up
3 to 5 minutes
*chromatic scales,
major/minor scales
arpeggios*

Technical exercises
5 to 25 minutes

Working sections separately
15 to 45 minutes

Play for your pleasure
5 to 10 minutes
*The current piece
An old pieces*

Session structure in order to prepare to play in front of an **audience**

Approximately one to two weeks before playing in front of an audience, you can follow the following routine ...

1ˢᵗ session of the day

WARM UP
3 à 5 minutes

METRONOME
slow x 1

MARATHON

METRONOME
fast x 1

METRONOME
slow x 2

2ⁿᵈ session of the day

Cold playing
the first piece you have to play

without interruption and without a break, you play

second piece

and you continue to chain together everything you will have to play during a concert or at a competition

TIPS

Don't hesitate to record yourself to identify your ticks and remove them.

You can switch between the first and second piece every other day.

SUMMARY OF TECHNIQUES

LEARNING NOTES

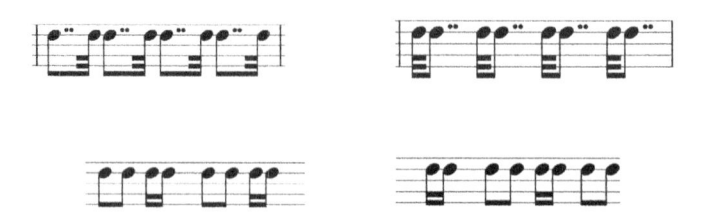

VIRTUOSITY: BACK-NIBBLING

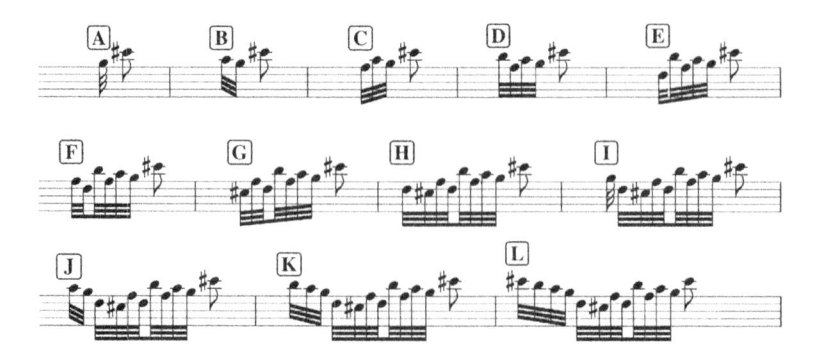

Each iteration must be successfully completed 3 times in a row before moving on to the next one.

SPEEDING UP THE TEMPO OF A PIECE

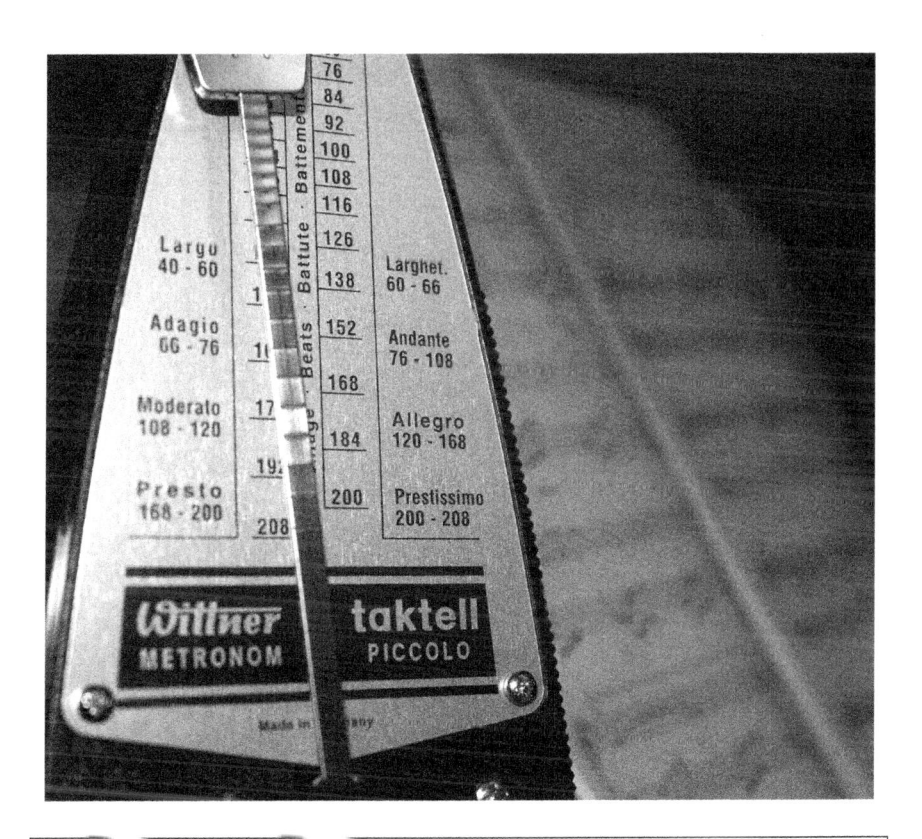

Technique 1
Accelerate gradually with the metronome: play the piece or section with the metronome starting very slowly and increasing the tempo with the metronome little by little. Be demanding about the regularity of the pulse.

Technique 2 (more difficult)
Accelerate with the metronome using the +10 → -5 rule

WORK TO ENSURE REGULARITY

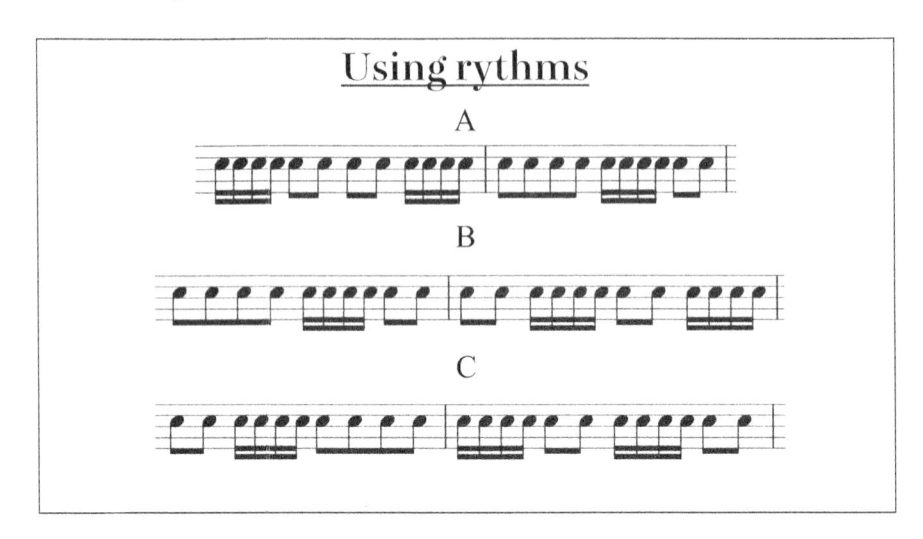

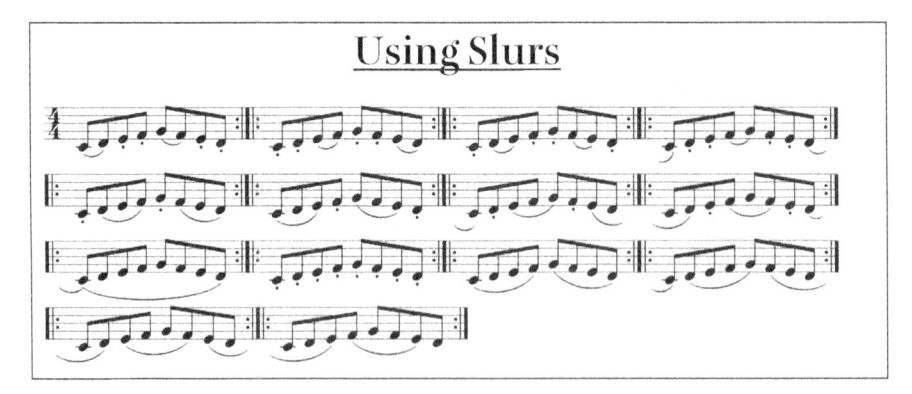

Using rythms

A

B

C

Using Slurs

Using the metronome at an unpleasant speed

(2-3 notches below the speed at which you are comfortable)

THE MARATHON
TRAINING TO PLAY IN FRONT OF AN AUDIENCE

> **Whole piece without interruption**
> **x3 in a row**

and, when you've got it right :

> **x 5 minimum**
> **You stop when you succeed**
> **3 times in a row without error**

TRAINING TO PLAY IN FRONT OF AN AUDIENCE

MARATHON VARIATION

PREVIOUS WORK

BUT INSTEAD OF 3X ERROR-FREE,

YOU HAVE TO PLAY :

5X ERROR-FREE

OR

8X ERROR-FREE
(MORE AVANCED)

WORKSHEETS

WORKSHEET
NAME OF THE PIECE: .... Date ....

Mark out the work already done

- Rythms

- Slurs

- Back-nibbling

- Metronome workouts :

    Classic   +10 –5   unpleasant speed -2 notches

- Marathon : ...   X3   X5   X8

---

other:

WORKSHEET
NAME OF THE PIECE: .... Date ....

Mark out the work already done

- Rythms

- Slurs

- Back-nibbling

- Metronome workouts :

    Classic   +10 –5   unpleasant speed -2 notches

- Marathon : ...   X3   X5   X8

---

other:

WORKSHEET

NAME OF THE PIECE: .... Date ....

Mark out the work already done

- Rythms

- Slurs

- Back-nibbling

- Metronome workouts :

    Classic   +10 −5   unpleasant speed -2 notches

- Marathon : ...   X3   X5   X8

---

other:

WORKSHEET
NAME OF THE PIECE: .... Date ....

Mark out the work already done

- Rythms

- Slurs

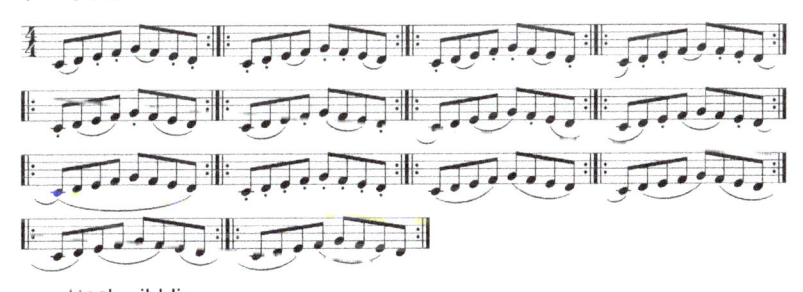

- Back-nibbling

- Metronome workouts :

  | Classic | +10 –5   unpleasant speed -2 notches

- Marathon : ...   X3   X5   X8

other:

WORKSHEET
NAME OF THE PIECE: .... Date ....

Mark out the work already done

- Rythms

- Slurs

- Back-nibbling

- Metronome workouts :

    | Classic | | +10 –5 | | unpleasant speed -2 notches |

- Marathon : ...   X3   X5   X8

---

other:

WORKSHEET
NAME OF THE PIECE: .... Date ....

Mark out the work already done

- Rythms

- Slurs

- Back-nibbling

- Metronome workouts :

    | Classic | | +10 −5 | | unpleasant speed -2 notches |

- Marathon : ...   X3   X5   X8

---

other:

WORKSHEET
NAME OF THE PIECE: .... Date ....

Mark out the work already done

- Rythms

- Slurs

- Back-nibbling

- Metronome workouts :

    | Classic | | +10 −5 | | unpleasant speed -2 notches |

- Marathon : ...   X3   X5   X8

---

other:

WORKSHEET

NAME OF THE PIECE: .... Date ....

Mark out the work already done

- Rythms

- Slurs

- Back-nibbling

- Metronome workouts :

    Classic   +10 −5   unpleasant speed -2 notches

- Marathon : ...   X3   X5   X8

---

other:

WORKSHEET
NAME OF THE PIECE: .... Date ....

Mark out the work already done

- Rythms

- Slurs

- Back-nibbling

- Metronome workouts :

    | Classic | | +10 −5 | | unpleasant speed -2 notches |

- Marathon : ... X3 X5 X8

---

other:

WORKSHEET
NAME OF THE PIECE: .... Date ....

Mark out the work already done

- Rythms

- Slurs

- Back-nibbling

- Metronome workouts :

    Classic   +10 –5   unpleasant speed -2 notches

- Marathon : ...   X3   X5   X8

other:

WORKSHEET
NAME OF THE PIECE: .... Date ....

Mark out the work already done

- Rythms

- Slurs

- Back-nibbling

- Metronome workouts :

    | Classic | | +10 –5 | | unpleasant speed -2 notches |

- Marathon : ...   X3   X5   X8

---

other:

If you want the .pdf file of the workout page

make a comment on Amazon, capture the screen when the comment is published and send it by mail to:
virtuose.instrumental@gmail.com

Do not hesitate to contact us if you have spotted an error or if you want to make a suggestion. We will correct the error, or we will be inspired by your suggestions in a new edition.

You will then receive the new edition **free of charge** as soon as it comes out, in pdf format, directly in your mailbox.

Contact mail
virtuose.instrumental@gmail.com

Printed in Great Britain
by Amazon